the art of slow cooking with

VersaWARE™

From Savory Entrées to Sweet Desserts,
Gourmet Recipes for Delicious Dishes

amy merydith

Pascoe Publishing, Inc.
Rocklin, California

Published in the United States of America by
Pascoe Publishing, Inc.

Printed in China

contents

CHAPTER 4: *Side Dishes*

CHAPTER 5: *Desserts*

1

Introduction — Using Your VersaWare™ Slow Cooker

Welcome to the newest innovation in cooking technology – the VersaWare™ slow cooker with ETC™ stoneware, from Rival, the makers of the Crock-Pot® slow cooker. What makes this new slow cooker so exciting? The unique ETC™ stoneware has a special formulation that can withstand extreme temperature changes – giving you the most versatile and convenient stoneware cooking appliance. Before each use, coat the inside of the stoneware with oil or butter to make clean-up easier. Use your ETC™ stoneware to prepare foods, slow cook in the base unit, store leftovers in the refrigerator and reheat them on the stove. The unique design and detachable cord allows you to go from countertop to tabletop to serve your guests in elegant fashion.

Your new VersaWare™ slow cooker is the ideal appliance for any number of cooking methods. You can braise, roast, sauté, and stew foods inside your ETC™ stoneware, automatically eliminating the need for many pots and pans, saving hours of clean-up. For example, a typical recipe may require four separate pans: one pan to sauté onions or garlic, an oven-proof pan for roasting the onions with other vegetables or meats, a small sauce pan for preparing gravy and, finally, yet another pan or platter for serving. Your VersaWare™ slow cooker streamlines all of those steps. You can sauté, roast, prepare sauces, serve and store leftovers – using only your ETC™ stoneware!

Many foods are best when prepared by slow cooking. Beef, pork, poultry and vegetables become moist, tender and juicy through the slow-cooking process. Whether you enjoy the sweetness of caramelized onions or the most flavorful roasts imaginable, the VersaWare™ slow cooker is the perfect solution for every occasion. From hot to cold, or cold to hot, your VersaWare™ slow cooker will serve you well. Have fun exploring all the different ways you can use your VersaWare™ slow cooker!

Sautéing with Your VersaWare™ Slow Cooker

Sautéing is a quick and easy method of food preparation and can be used to quick-cook vegetables, seafood or meat. Sautéing uses a small amount of oil or butter to create a rich flavor caused by the sugars which develop through caramelization when browning. Toss foods periodically as they sauté to ensure even cooking and color. Sautéed foods, such as roasted red and yellow peppers, typically cook quickly and are the perfect companions to simple chops and grilled cuts of beef.

PLEASE NOTE: When using on a gas stove, the ETC™ stoneware may be placed directly on the stovetop. When using on an electric stove (smoothtop or coil), a heat diffuser MUST ALWAYS

be used with the ETC™ stoneware. If the heat diffuser is not used on an electric stovetop, the stoneware could be damaged. Please see pages 9 and 10 for instructions on how to use a heat diffuser with your stoneware. Placing the ETC™ stoneware on high heat when using it on the stovetop may also damage the stoneware. Always begin stovetop cooking on low heat before increasing to medium or medium low temperature.

Roasting with Your VersaWare™ Slow Cooker

Roasting is a dry method of cooking in the oven. Because roasting will not tenderize the finished product, meats that are to be roasted should be tender and well marbled. They are usually cut from the rib, loin or leg sections. When roasting, seasoning is especially important to give a highly seasoned crust associated with a good roast. Choose small roasts with a thin fat layer to add richness and moisture. Piercing roasts with garlic studs also adds great flavor.

Braising with Your VersaWare™ Slow Cooker

Braised meats are first browned on the stovetop and then cooked in a liquid that serves as a sauce for the meat. Braising can be used for both tender cuts, such as those from the beef or pork loin or rib, or tougher cuts such as those from the beef chuck or shank. When braising or stewing, choose a cut of beef that is well-marbled with even strains of fat running through the meat for optimum flavor. The flavor of a braised dish is a function of quality of the cooking liquid, the vegetables, and the herbs and spices that season the meat as it cooks. Braised meats can also be marinated before they are cooked to tenderize and add flavor. Braised meats are done when they are tender but do not fall apart.

Simmering with Your VersaWare™ Slow Cooker

Simmering foods for a long period of time brings out the deepest and most inviting flavors. Many soups, stews and chowders can be simmered in your VersaWare™ slow cooker. Fresh or corned beef brisket, or fresh or cured hams are often simmered whole. Simmering cured meats will drain out the excess salt, leaving the prepared meat with a delicious flavor. Simmer meats until they are very tender and cooked well-done. Your VersaWare™ slow cooker is perfect for cooking corned beef and cabbage on St. Patrick's Day, and a flavorful chowder or a comforting harvest soup is simple and easy any day of the year.

Crock•Pot® VersaWARE. Slow Cooker

WARNING: TO PREVENT DAMAGE TO YOUR ETC™ STONEWARE, YOU MUST FOLLOW THE SAFEGUARDS BELOW.

ALWAYS use the enclosed HEAT DIFFUSER when cooking on ELECTRIC STOVETOPS or breakage may result.

DO NOT use on HIGH HEAT on the stovetop.

DO NOT heat empty stoneware on stovetop burners. Always ensure there is liquid or food inside the stoneware.

ALWAYS begin stovetop cooking on low heat before increasing to medium or medium low temperature.

ALWAYS coat the bottom of the stoneware with a minimum of 2 tablespoons of oil when sautéing or browning on the stovetop.

ALWAYS stir food often when cooking on the stovetop.

NEVER freeze water or water based foods in the stoneware. It may result in cracking of the stoneware.

DO NOT use metal utensils with the stoneware to protect against scratches.

How to Use Heat Diffuser with ETC™ Stoneware

— ETC™ stoneware

— Heat Diffuser
*cross-supports facing up

— Electric Stovetop

Note: when using on an electric stovetop (smoothtop or coil) a heat diffuser MUST ALWAYS be used with the ETC™ Stoneware.

2

Soups & Chowders

Tuscan Eggplant & Fresh Herb Ragoût

1 medium eggplant, cut into 1/2-inch cubes
2 cups ripe tomato, chopped
1 cup carrots, sliced
15 ounce can white beans, drained
8 ounce can red kidney beans, drained and rinsed
1 cup white onion, chopped
1 cup celery, sliced
3 cloves garlic, minced
3 cups vegetable broth
6 ounce can tomato paste
1 tablespoon fresh oregano leaves, finely chopped
1 tablespoon fresh basil leaves, finely chopped
1 tablespoon flat leaf parsley, finely chopped
1/4 teaspoon salt
1/4 teaspoon freshly ground black pepper
1/4 teaspoon cayenne pepper
1 bay leaf

Combine the eggplant, tomatoes, carrots, white beans, kidney beans, onion, celery and garlic in the ETC™ stoneware and toss lightly to mix all of the ingredients. Place the stoneware in the heating base unit and set on High setting. In a medium mixing bowl, combine the vegetable broth, tomato paste, oregano, basil, parsley, salt, pepper, cayenne and bay leaf. Pour the broth and herbs over the vegetables and stir once. Cover and cook on High setting for 2½ to 4 hours or on Low setting for 7 to 8 hours. Discard the bay leaf before serving. Makes 6 servings.

Penne Pasta Zuppa

15 ounce can white beans
2 small red potatoes, cubed
1 carrot, peeled and diced
2 leeks, thinly sliced
2 ripe tomatoes, diced
1/4 pound fresh green beans, washed, stemmed and diced
2 medium yellow squash, diced
2 fresh sage leaves, minced
1 teaspoon salt
1/2 teaspoon coarsely ground black pepper
2 quarts water
4 ounces penne pasta, uncooked
Romano cheese for garnish

Combine the beans, potatoes, carrots, leeks, tomatoes, green beans, squash, sage, salt and pepper in the ETC™ stoneware. Add 2 quarts of water and set the heating base unit to High. Cover and cook for 1 hour, stirring occasionally. Turn the heat setting to Low and cook, covered, for 5 to 8 hours. Stir occasionally. Add the penne pasta, turn to High setting and cook an additional 30 minutes. To serve, ladle the soup into 6 individual bowls and sprinkle Romano cheese over each serving for garnish. Serve immediately. Serves 6.

Red Bliss Potato & Leek Clam Chowder

4 slices bacon, cut into 1 inch pieces
2 6 ounce cans minced clams, drained, liquid reserved
2 cups red bliss potatoes, peeled and cut into 1/2-inch
    cubes
1 cup leeks, finely chopped
1 cup celery, chopped
2 carrots, peeled and finely chopped
1 teaspoon sugar
1 teaspoon salt
1/2 teaspoon black pepper
3 cups heavy cream
2 cups water
1 cup dry milk powder
1/3 cup flour
1 cup chilled water
ground paprika

If using a Gas stove, use the ETC™ stoneware to sauté the bacon on low heat for a few minutes and then turn the heat up to medium until crisp. Do not use on high heat.

If using an Electric stove, use the ETC™ stoneware with the heat diffuser (see page 10), to sauté the bacon until crisp over medium low heat. Do not use on high heat.

Remove the bacon with a slotted spoon and set aside on a paper towel to drain. Cool and reserve in the refrigerator. Place the clams in a small mixing bowl and cover with plastic wrap. Chill in the refrigerator while preparing the soup. Place the reserved clam liquid in the stoneware and add the potatoes, leeks, celery, carrots, sugar, salt and pepper. Mix thoroughly to blend. Stir in the cream and add 1 cup of the water.

Place the stoneware in the heating base unit. Cover and cook on High setting for 2 to 4 hours or on Low setting for 6 hours. In a medium mixing bowl, combine the dry milk and flour. Gradually whisk in 1 cup of chilled water. Add this mixture to the soup and stir to combine. Cover and cook on High setting 20 to 30 minutes, or until thickened and very smooth. Meanwhile, remove the bacon from the refrigerator to come to room temperature. Stir occasionally as the soup simmers. Add the clams and cook for an additional 5 minutes. To serve, ladle the soup into 6 individual bowls, dust each with the paprika and crumble the bacon evenly over each serving. Makes 6 to 8 servings.

Mediterranean Tomato, Oregano & Orzo Soup

2 tablespoons extra virgin olive oil
1 large yellow onion, cut into wedges
2 cups butternut squash, peeled and cut into cubes
1/2 cup zucchini, cleaned and sliced
1 cup carrots, peeled and julienne-cut
3 1/2 cups fresh tomatoes, peeled and hand-crushed
1 tablespoon fresh bay leaves, minced
1 tablespoon fresh oregano leaves, chopped
15 ounce can garbanzo beans, drained and rinsed
2 cups chicken broth
1 clove garlic, minced
1 teaspoon ground cumin
1/2 teaspoon salt
3/4 teaspoon ground allspice
1/4 teaspoon freshly ground black pepper
1 1/2 cups dried orzo pasta

If using a Gas stove, add the oil and onions to the ETC™ stoneware and cook over low heat. Do not use on high heat. **If using an Electric stove,** use the ETC™ stoneware with the heat diffuser (see page 10). Add the oil and onions and cook over medium-low heat. Do not use on high heat.

Stir the onions occasionally until the onions are translucent and soft, about 10 minutes. Add the butternut and zucchini squash, carrots, tomatoes, bay leaves and oregano. Sauté for an additional 25 to 30 minutes, stirring occasionally as the vegetables soften. Combine all of the ingredients except the orzo pasta in the ETC™ stoneware. Transfer the stoneware to the heating base unit. Cover and set on High setting for 2 to 4 hours or on Low setting for 5 to 7 hours. Add the orzo and set on High setting. Cover and continue cooking for 30 to 45 minutes. Serves 6.

Caramelized French Onion Soup

2 tablespoons butter
2 extra-large sweet onions, cut into 1/2-inch-thick slices
1 cup dry white wine
4 cups beef or vegetable broth, divided
1 cup water
1/2 tablespoon fresh thyme leaves, minced
6 cups large seasoned croutons
1 cup Swiss cheese, shredded

If using a Gas Stove, use the ETC™ stoneware to caramelize the onions by combining the butter and onions over very low heat. Do not use on high heat.

If using an Electric Stove, use the ETC™ stoneware with heat diffuser (see page 10) to caramelize the onions by combining the butter and onions over very low heat. Do not use on high heat.

Stir every 7 to 8 minutes and remove the onions when they are soft and caramelized, about 45 to 50 minutes. Add the wine and let the liquid reduce almost completely, about 15 minutes.

To prepare the soup add the broth, water, and thyme to the caramelized onions in the stoneware. Transfer the stoneware to the heating base unit. Cover and set on High setting for 2½ hours or until the soup is thoroughly heated. Just prior to serving, ladle soup into individual, oven-proof soup bowls. Place croutons over the top of the soup and sprinkle cheese over the croutons. Preheat the oven broiler and place the bowls on top shelf of oven. Broil for 3 to 5 minutes, or until the cheese is melted and golden. Serve immediately. Serves 6.

Sweet & Sour Chicken Soup

2 tablespoons extra virgin olive oil
2 pounds boneless, skinless chicken thighs, cut into 1-inch
    cubes
15 ounce can tomato sauce
1 teaspoon ground paprika
1 teaspoon crystallized ginger, chopped
1/4 cup dark brown sugar, packed
1 teaspoon salt
1/2 cup dry red wine
1/3 cup light corn syrup
2 tablespoons rice vinegar
2 medium carrots, peeled & sliced
1 medium onion, peeled and diced
1 small green bell pepper, cored, seeded and diced
1 small yellow bell pepper, cored, seeded and diced
1/2 cup fresh or canned pineapple chunks
3 cups long grain white rice, steamed

If using a Gas stove, add the oil to the ETC™ stoneware and heat over low heat, increasing the temperature to medium after a few minutes. Do not use on high heat.

If using an Electric stove, use the ETC™ stoneware with heat diffuser (see page 10) to heat the oil over low heat, increasing the temperature to medium after a few minutes. Do not use on high heat.

Once the oil is hot, brown one-half of the chicken pieces on each side, about 3 to 5 minutes, turning once. Remove the chicken with a slotted spoon and repeat with the remaining chicken. Return all of the chicken to the stoneware and add the tomato sauce, paprika, ginger, brown sugar, salt, wine, corn syrup, vinegar, carrots, onion, peppers and pineapple. Transfer the stoneware to the heating base unit. Cover and set on High setting 2 to 4 hours or on Low setting for 5 to 7 hours, or until the chicken is very tender and the sauce is smooth. To serve, spoon ½ cup of rice into each of 6 individual bowls. Ladle equal portions of soup over the rice and serve immediately. Serves 6.

Northwest Beef & Vegetable Soup

2 tablespoons extra virgin olive oil
1 pound lean stew beef, fat removed and cut into 1-inch cubes
1 clove garlic, minced
1 medium onion, chopped
15 ounce can white beans, drained and rinsed
1 buttercup or butternut squash, peeled and diced
1 turnip, peeled and diced
1 large potato, peeled and diced
2 stalks celery, sliced
3 1/2 cups canned tomatoes, peeled and crushed
2 tablespoons fresh basil, minced
1 teaspoon freshly ground pepper
1 1/2 teaspoons salt
8 cups water

If using a Gas stove, add the oil to the ETC™ stoneware and heat over low heat, increasing the temperature to medium after a few minutes. Do not use on high heat.

If using an Electric stove, use the ETC™ stoneware with heat diffuser (see page 10) to heat the oil over low heat, increasing the temperature to medium after a few minutes. Do not use on high heat.

Once the oil is hot, sear 4 or 5 pieces of beef at a time on all sides, turning each piece as it browns. Sear the last batch of beef with the onions and garlic. Return all the seared beef back to the stoneware, along with the beans, squash, turnip, potato, celery, and tomatoes. Gently stir to combine ingredients. Add the seasonings and pour the water over all. Mix well. Transfer the stoneware to the heating base unit. Cover and set on High setting for 2 hours. Turn to Low setting and cook an additional 3 to 6 hours. Stir occasionally and adjust seasonings as needed. Serves 6 to 8.

Sweet Italian Sausage & Vegetable Soup

2 tablespoons extra virgin olive oil or vegetable oil
1 pound sweet Italian sausage, casings removed
1 stalk celery, finely chopped
1 medium yellow squash, peeled and diced
1 small white onion, peeled and sliced thin
3 cups beef broth
1 medium tomato, peeled and freshly crushed
1 teaspoon salt
2 teaspoons fresh basil leaves, chopped
1 teaspoon fresh oregano leaves, chopped
1 teaspoon freshly ground black pepper
1 cup Romano cheese, freshly grated

If using a Gas stove, add the oil to the ETC™ stoneware and heat over low heat, increasing the temperature to medium after a few minutes. Do not use on high heat.

If using an Electric stove, use the ETC™ stoneware with heat diffuser (see page 10) to heat the oil over low heat, increasing the temperature to medium after a few minutes. Do not use on high heat.

Once the oil is hot, brown and crumble the sausage until no pink remains, about 10 minutes. Drain any fat that accumulates. Add the celery, squash and onion and sauté for 4 minutes, stirring continuously. Combine all of the ingredients except the grated cheese in the stoneware. Transfer the stoneware to the heating base unit. Cover and set on High setting for 2 to 3 hours or on Low setting for 4 to 6 hours. Add additional salt and pepper to taste. Ladle the soup into bowls and top each serving with the Romano cheese. Serves 6.

Seafood & Tomato Herb Ragoût

28 ounce can crushed tomatoes, with juices
1 cup water
1 teaspoon salt
8 ounce can tomato sauce
1 leek, chopped
1/2 cup celery, chopped
1 cup white wine
1/4 cup extra virgin olive oil
3 cloves garlic, minced
1/3 cup fresh parsley, chopped
1 small green bell pepper, cored, seeded and chopped
1 tablespoon fresh thyme, chopped
2 tablespoons fresh basil, chopped
1 tablespoons fresh oregano, chopped
1/2 teaspoon ground paprika
1/4 teaspoon crushed red pepper

1 pound tilapia fillets, cut into 1 inch cubes
1 dozen medium prawns or shrimp, cleaned, deveined
     and shelled
1 dozen medium scallops, cleaned
fresh parsley for garnish

Combine all of the ingredients except the seafood in the ETC™ stoneware. Stir to blend. Cover and cook in the heating base unit on High setting for 2 to 4 hours or on Low setting for 5 to 8 hours. Add the seafood and turn the heat setting to High. Cook for an additional 10-12 minutes or until the seafood is completely cooked, stirring occasionally. Add the parsley to garnish. Serves 6 to 8.

Asian Sugar Snap Pea Soup

2 tablespoons peanut or canola oil
2 green onions, chopped
4 to 5 new potatoes, coarsely chopped
1 medium carrot, peeled and sliced thin
1 stalk celery, sliced thin
1 leek, sliced thin
1 tablespoon fresh-squeezed lemon juice
1 tablespoon soy sauce
1 teaspoon ground coriander
1 teaspoon ground cumin
1 teaspoon pure prepared horseradish
1/8 teaspoon cayenne pepper
1 teaspoon salt
1/2 teaspoon ground black pepper
5 cups water
2 cups broccoli, washed and cut into florets
1 cup fresh sugar snap peas, shelled rinsed and drained
4 cups steamed white rice

If using a Gas stove, add the oil, onions, potato, carrot, celery, and leeks to the ETC™ stoneware and sauté over low heat. Do not use on high heat.

If using an Electric stove, use the ETC™ stoneware with heat diffuser (see page 10) to sauté the oil, onions, potato, carrot, celery, and leeks over low heat. Do not use on high heat.

Sauté the vegetables for 10–12 minutes, or until they begin to soften. Transfer the stoneware to the heating base unit. Add all of the ingredients except the broccoli, snap peas and rice to the sautéed vegetables in the stoneware. Cover and set on High setting for 2 to 3 hours or on Low setting for 4 to 6 hours. Fifteen minutes before serving, stir in the broccoli and sugar snap peas. To serve, portion the rice into 4 bowls. Ladle the soup over the rice and serve immediately. Serves 4.

Cannellini Minestrone Soup

12 ounce can tomato-vegetable juice
1 cup green onions, chopped
1 cup carrots, peeled and chopped
1 cup celery, chopped
1 cup potatoes, chopped
14 1/2 ounce can tomatoes, diced, with juice
2 cups escarole, cut into ribbons
2 tablespoons fresh chives, chopped
1 tablespoon fresh parsley, freshly chopped
1/4 teaspoon salt
1/4 teaspoon pepper, freshly ground
1/4 cup cannellini beans, uncooked
4 cups chicken broth
2 ounces ditilini noodles

In the ETC™ stoneware, add the tomato juice, onions, carrots, celery, potatoes, tomatoes, escarole, chives, parsley, salt, pepper and beans. Pour the chicken broth over the mixture and stir well to combine. Cover and cook on High setting for 2 to 4 hours or on Low setting for 5 to 7 hours. Twenty minutes prior to serving, add the ditilini noodles and stir again. The noodles will be perfectly cooked when ready to serve. Serves 6.

French Beef Bourguignon

---

2 tablespoons vegetable oil
2 pounds boneless beef chuck, cut into 1-inch pieces
2 cups carrots, cut into thin pieces about 4-inches in
    length
2 stalks celery, sliced
1 small yellow onion, peeled and diced
14 1/2 ounce can diced tomatoes, undrained
1 cup white button mushrooms, chopped
1 cup dry red wine
1 teaspoon salt
1 tablespoon fresh thyme leaves, chopped
1 teaspoon fresh basil, minced
1 teaspoon dry mustard
1/4 teaspoon freshly ground pepper
1/4 cup water
2 tablespoons flour

If using a Gas stove, add the oil to the ETC™ stoneware and heat over low heat, increasing the temperature to medium after a few minutes. Do not use on high heat.

If using an Electric stove, use the ETC™ stoneware with heat diffuser (see page 10) to heat the oil over low heat, increasing the temperature to medium after a few minutes. Do not use on high heat.

Once the oil is hot, sear 4 or 5 pieces of beef at a time on all sides, turning each piece as it browns. Repeat with the remaining beef until it has all been browned. Return all of the beef to the stoneware and transfer the stoneware to the heating base unit. Add the carrots, celery, onion, tomatoes, mushrooms, wine, salt, thyme, basil, mustard and pepper. Cover and cook on High setting for 2 to 4 hours or on Low setting for 5 to 8 hours, or until the vegetables and beef are very tender and the sauce is rich. Thirty minutes before serving, combine the water and flour in a small bowl until smooth. Turn the heat setting to High. Gradually add the flour and water to the soup and stir until the sauce thickens, about 3 to 5 minutes. Heat through and serve. Makes 8 servings.

Creamy Crab Bisque

3 cups fresh crab meat, flaked and picked
4 cups heavy cream
3 tablespoons unsalted butter
2 teaspoons lemon zest
1 teaspoon fresh squeezed lemon juice
1/4 teaspoon ground nutmeg
1/4 teaspoon ground allspice
3 tablespoons dry red wine
1/2 cup prepared mandlen (soup nuts), ground to make
    crumbs
salt and ground black pepper to taste

Combine the crab, cream, butter, lemon zest, lemon juice, nutmeg and allspice in the ETC™ stoneware and blend well. Cover and cook on Low setting in the heating base unit for 1 to 2 hours. Just before serving, stir in the wine. Add the mandlen crumbs to thicken the soup and stir again. Continue cooking for 10 minutes. Season with salt and pepper. Serves 6 to 8.

Tuscany Bean & Prosciutto Soup

2 tablespoons unsalted butter
4 slices uncooked prosciutto (you may substitute bacon, if desired)
1 cup navy beans, rinsed and sorted
1/2 cup lima beans, rinsed and sorted
1 yellow onion, peeled and finely chopped
3 cups water
1 teaspoon salt
1 teaspoon ground cumin
1/2 teaspoon ground paprika
1 teaspoon freshly ground black pepper
1 tablespoon fresh cilantro, chopped
2 – 15 ounce cans diced tomatoes, with juices
1/4 cup Parmesan cheese, shredded

If using a Gas stove, use the ETC™ stoneware to sauté the prosciutto on low for a few minutes and then turn the heat up to medium until the prosciutto is crisp. Do not use on high heat.

If using an Electric stove, use the ETC™ stoneware with heat diffuser (see page 10) to sauté the prosciutto on low for a few minutes then turn the heat up to medium until the prosciutto is crisp. Do not use on high heat.

Remove the proscuitto with a slotted spoon and set aside on a paper towel to drain. Transfer the prosciutto to a cutting board and chop into small pieces. Combine the prosciutto, navy beans, lima beans, onion, water, salt, cumin, paprika, pepper and cilantro in the stoneware and mix well to blend. Transfer the stoneware to the heating base unit. Cover and cook on Low setting for 3 to 5 hours. Add the tomatoes, stir well and cook on High setting for an additional 30 to 40 minutes, or until the soup is heated through. Garnish with Parmesan cheese when serving. Makes 6 servings.

Roasted Corn & Red Pepper Chowder

---

2 tablespoons extra virgin olive oil
2 cups fresh corn kernels (you may substitute frozen,
    thawed corn, if desired)
1 red bell pepper, cored, seeded and diced
2 green onions, sliced
4 cups chicken broth
2 baking potatoes, peeled and diced
1 teaspoon salt
1/2 teaspoon freshly ground black pepper
13 ounce can evaporated milk
2 tablespoons flat leaf parsley, minced

If using a Gas stove, add the oil, corn, and red peppers to the ETC™ stoneware and sauté over low heat. Do not use on high heat.

If using an Electric stove, use the ETC™ stoneware with the heat diffuser (see page 10) to sauté the oil, corn, and red peppers over low heat. Do not use on high heat.

Sauté the vegetables until they are tender and lightly browned, about 7-8 minutes. Transfer the stoneware to the heating base unit. Add the green onions, broth, potatoes, salt and pepper to the stoneware and stir to combine. Cover and cook on High setting for 2 to 4 hours or on Low setting for 5 to 7 hours. Thirty minutes prior to serving, add the milk and blend well. Garnish with the parsley to serve. Serves 4.

Savory Chicken & Oregano Soup

2 – 15 ounce cans great northern or cannellini beans,
   drained
2 cups cooked chicken, chopped
1 medium onion, peeled and chopped
2 medium red peppers, seeded and chopped
4 ounce can diced green chilies
3 cloves garlic, minced
3 1/2 cups chicken broth
2 teaspoons ground cumin
1 teaspoon salt
1 tablespoon fresh oregano, minced

Combine all of the ingredients in the ETC™ stoneware and mix thoroughly. Cover and cook in the heating base unit on High setting for 3 to 5 hours or on Low setting for 6 to 8 hours. Makes 8 servings.

3

Main Dishes

Basil Chicken Merlot with Wild Mushrooms

4 tablespoons extra virgin olive oil, divided
3 pounds roasting chicken, cut into individual pieces,
    skinned
1 1/2 cups crimini mushrooms, cleaned and thickly sliced
1 medium yellow onion, diced
2 cloves garlic, minced
1 cup chicken broth
6 ounce can tomato paste
1/3 cup Merlot, or other dry red wine
1 teaspoon ground oregano
2 teaspoons granulated sugar
1/4 teaspoon salt
1/4 teaspoon freshly ground pepper
2 tablespoons fresh basil, minced
3 cups cooked ziti pasta, drained
Romano cheese for garnish

If using a Gas stove, add 2 tablespoons oil to the ETC™ stoneware and heat over low heat, increasing the temperature to medium after a few minutes. Do not use on high heat.

If using an Electric stove, use the ETC™ stoneware with the heat diffuser (see page 10) to heat 2 tablespoons oil over low heat, increasing the temperature to medium after a few minutes. Do not use on high heat.

Once the oil is hot, brown one-half of the chicken pieces on each side, about 3 to 5 minutes, turning once. Remove the chicken with a slotted spoon and repeat with the remaining chicken. Set all of the browned chicken aside.

Heat the remaining oil and add the mushrooms, onion and garlic. Sauté the vegetables for 7 to 8 minutes or until the onions are soft.

Transfer the stoneware to the heating base unit. Arrange the chicken pieces on top of the vegetables. In a medium mixing bowl, combine the broth, tomato paste, wine, oregano, sugar, salt and pepper. Pour the sauce over the chicken. Cover and cook on High setting for 2 to 4 hours or on Low setting for 5 to 7 hours. Stir in the fresh basil. Spoon the cooked pasta into a deep, large serving bowl or platter. Ladle the chicken and mushrooms over the pasta and spoon the extra sauce over all. Garnish with the Romano cheese. Makes 4 to 6 servings.

East Indian Curried Chicken with Capers & Brown Rice

2 cups ripe plum tomatoes, diced
1 cup canned artichoke hearts, drained and chopped
1 cup chicken broth
1 medium red onion, chopped
1/4 cup capers, drained
1/3 cup dry white wine
2 tablespoons quick cooking tapioca
2 teaspoons curry powder
1/2 teaspoon ground thyme
1/4 teaspoon salt
1/4 teaspoon freshly ground black pepper
1 1/2 pounds chicken breasts, boneless and skinless
4 cups hot, steamed brown rice

Combine the tomatoes, artichoke hearts, chicken broth, onion, capers and wine in the ETC™ stoneware. Add the tapioca, curry, thyme, salt and pepper and stir well to combine. Add the chicken and spoon some of the sauce over the chicken breast portions. Cover and cook in the heating base unit on High setting for 2 to 3 hours or on Low setting for 3 to 5 hours. To serve, spoon the chicken and vegetables over the rice. Serves 6.

Autumn Herbed Chicken with Fennel and Squash

---

2 tablespoons extra virgin olive oil
3-4 pounds chicken thighs
salt and ground black pepper to taste
all purpose flour
1 fennel bulb, thinly sliced
1/2 butternut squash, peeled, seeded, and cut into 3/4
    inch cubes
1 teaspoon dried thyme leaves
3/4 cup shelled walnuts (optional)
3/4 cup chicken stock
1/2 cup apple cider or juice
1/4 cup fresh basil leaves cut into ribbons
2 teaspoons fresh rosemary, finely minced

If using a Gas stove, add the oil to the ETC™ stoneware and heat over low heat, increasing the temperature to medium after a few minutes. Do not use on high heat.

If using an Electric stove, use the ETC™ stoneware with the heat diffuser (see page 10) to heat the oil over low heat, increasing the temperature to medium after a few minutes. Do not use on high heat.

Preheat the oven to 325°F.

Season the chicken on all sides with salt and pepper, then lightly coat with flour. Once the oil is hot, brown the chicken thighs in batches on each side, about 3 to 5 minutes, turning once. Remove the chicken with a slotted spoon and repeat with the remaining chicken. Place all of the browned chicken in the stoneware. Add the fennel, squash and thyme to the stoneware. Stir to combine ingredients. Add the walnuts, chicken stock and apple cider. Cover and braise in the oven for 1½ to 2 hours. Serve over rice or pasta and garnish with the basil ribbons and fresh rosemary. Makes 6 servings.

Stuffed Lamb Roast with Rosemary & Mint

3 pounds lamb roast, deboned
1 medium onion, finely chopped
2 tablespoons unsalted butter, melted
1/2 cup unseasoned bread crumbs
1 egg, beaten
1 teaspoon salt
1 teaspoon freshly ground black pepper
1 tablespoon fresh rosemary, minced
1 tablespoon fresh mint, minced
1 tablespoon lemon zest, grated
3 cloves garlic, minced
2 stalks celery, thinly sliced
1 medium carrot, peeled and finely chopped
salt and pepper to taste
2 tablespoons vegetable oil

Remove the excess fat from the lamb roast and flatten the lamb as much as possible. In a medium mixing bowl, combine the remaining ingredients, except the salt, pepper and vegetable oil, and toss to mix well. Spread the stuffing down the middle of the lamb, as evenly as possible, and roll the lamb in jelly-roll fashion. Fasten the lamb with skewers or string. Season the outside of the lamb with salt and pepper to taste.

If using a Gas stove, add the oil to the ETC™ stoneware and heat over low heat, increasing the temperature to medium after a few minutes. Do not use on high heat.

If using an Electric stove, use the ETC™ stoneware with the heat diffuser (see page 10) to heat the oil over low heat, increasing the temperature to medium after a few minutes. Do not use on high heat.

Once the oil is hot, sear the lamb on all sides until brown, about 3 to 4 minutes per side. Transfer the stoneware to the heating base unit. Cook for 2 to 4 hours on High setting or 5 to 8 hours on Low setting. Remove the lamb and let it rest for 15 minutes before slicing. Pour the natural juices over the lamb to serve. Serves 8.

Mediterranean Lamb Shanks

2 tablespoons extra virgin olive oil
3 pounds lamb shanks
salt and ground black pepper
all purpose flour
1 medium red onion, chopped
2 garlic cloves, minced
1 large red bell pepper, seeded and sliced
1 medium eggplant, peeled and cut into 1/2 inch cubes
1 large tomato, seeded and chopped
1 teaspoon dried thyme
1/2 teaspoon dried rosemary
2 cinnamon sticks
2 cups red wine
1/2 cup calamata olives, pitted
2 tablespoons fresh parsley leaves, finely chopped

If using a Gas stove, add the oil to the ETC™ stoneware and heat over low heat, increasing the temperature to medium after a few minutes. Do not use on high heat.

If using an Electric stove, use the ETC™ stoneware with the heat diffuser (see page 10) to heat the oil over low heat, increasing the temperature to medium after a few minutes. Do not use on high heat.

Preheat the oven to 325°F.

Season the lamb on both sides with salt and pepper, then lightly coat with flour. Once the oil is hot, brown the lamb in batches 1 to 2 minutes per side and remove. Add the onion and garlic and cook an additional 3 to 4 minutes until the onion softens. Combine this mixture with the lamb, peppers, eggplant, tomato, herbs, cinnamon, and red wine in the stoneware. Stir to thoroughly combine ingredients. Cover the stoneware and braise in the oven 1 to 2 hours until the meat is cooked and tender. Remove the cinnamon sticks, garnish with olives and parsley and serve. Makes 6 servings.

Chicken Gumbo over Rice

5 tablespoons extra virgin olive oil
1/2 pound Italian sausage, cut into 1/4-inch slices
1/4 cup all purpose flour
1 cup onions, finely diced
1 cup celery, finely diced
1 cup green bell peppers, diced
1 teaspoon ground paprika
2 tablespoons jalapeños or Serrano peppers, minced
1 pound chicken breast, cut into 1/2 inch slices
1 cup chicken stock
1/2 cup white wine
1 1/2 cups fresh or frozen okra, cut into 1/4 inch slices
2 cups cooked brown or white rice

If using a Gas stove, add 2 tablespoons of the oil to the ETC™ stoneware and heat over low heat, increasing the temperature to medium after a few minutes. Do not use on high heat.

If using an Electric stove, use the ETC™ stoneware with the heat diffuser (see page 10) to heat 2 tablespoons of the oil over low heat, increasing the temperature to medium after a few minutes. Do not use on high heat.

Preheat the oven to 325°F.

Once the oil is hot, brown the sausage until no pink remains. Remove with a slotted spoon, drain the grease, reduce the heat to low and add the remaining oil. Add the flour and whisk. Cook until the flour has become a dark brown color but not burned. Add the onions, celery, peppers, paprika, chili peppers, and chicken breast. Stir to combine and sauté 7 to 8 minutes until the vegetables soften. Combine stock, wine and okra in the stoneware. Cover and braise in the oven 1½ to 2 hours until almost all of the liquid has evaporated. Serve over cooked rice. Makes 6 servings.

Roast Chicken with Peas, Prosciutto & Cream

2 1/2 pounds whole roasting chicken, cleaned and
     seasoned with salt and pepper
1 small white onion, finely chopped
5 ounces prosciutto, diced
1/2 cup dry white wine
10 ounce pkg. frozen peas
1/2 cup heavy cream
1 1/2 tablespoons cornstarch
2 tablespoons water
4 cups farfale pasta, cooked al dente

Combine the chicken, onion, prosciutto and wine in the ETC™ stoneware. Transfer the stoneware to the heating base unit. Cover and cook on High setting for 2½ to 4 hours or on Low setting 5 to 8 hours. During the last 30 minutes of cooking, add the frozen peas and heavy cream to the stoneware. Remove the chicken when done and no pink remains. Carve the meat and set aside on a warmed platter. Combine the cornstarch and water and add to the liquid in the stoneware. Return the stoneware to the heating base unit and heat on High setting until the sauce is thickened. To serve, spoon the pasta onto individual plates, place the chicken over the pasta and top each portion with sauce. Makes 6 servings.

Rolled Veal Roast with Tarragon Cream Gravy

---

1 tablespoon unsalted butter
1 tablespoon extra virgin olive oil
4 pounds boned, rolled and tied veal shoulder roast
8 crimini mushrooms, cleaned and quartered
6 medium carrots, peeled cut in half and cut lengthwise
2 tablespoons fresh tarragon, finely minced, divided
1/8 teaspoon freshly ground white pepper
1/4 cup fresh squeezed lemon juice
3/4 cup dry white wine
3 tablespoons cornstarch
1/3 cup whipping cream
salt and pepper to taste
lemon peel twists for garnish

If using a Gas stove, add the butter and oil to the ETC™ stoneware and heat over low heat, increasing the temperature to medium after a few minutes. Do not use on high heat.

If using an Electric stove, use the ETC™ stoneware with the heat diffuser (see page 10) to heat the butter and oil over low heat, increasing the temperature to medium after a few minutes. Do not use on high heat.

Once the butter and oil are hot, sear the veal roast on all sides, turning it to brown evenly. Place the stoneware in the heating base unit. Place the mushrooms and carrots around the roast. Sprinkle with 1 tablespoon of the tarragon and white pepper. Pour the lemon juice and dry wine over all. Cover and cook on High setting for 2 to 3 hours or on Low setting for 4 to 5 hours.

Transfer the roast to a carving board and let stand for 10 minutes. Carve into thick slices and set aside on a warm platter. With a slotted spoon, lift the carrots and mushrooms from the stoneware and arrange the vegetables around the veal slices. Cover with aluminum foil and keep warm. Turn the heating base unit to High. Whisk together the remaining tarragon, cornstarch and cream and add to the juices. Add salt and pepper to taste. Stir and cook as the gravy heats, about 6 to 8 minutes. To serve, pass the warm sauce at the table to pour over the veal and vegetables. Serves 6.

Pork Chops l'Orange

2 tablespoons extra virgin olive oil
8 thick cut pork chops
1/3 cup fresh squeezed orange juice
2 tablespoons clover honey
1 teaspoon salt
1 teaspoon brown sugar, packed
1 teaspoon orange zest
2 tablespoons cornstarch
1/4 cup water

If using a Gas stove, add the oil to the ETC™ stoneware and heat over low heat, increasing the temperature to medium after a few minutes. Do not use on high heat.

If using an Electric stove, use the ETC™ stoneware with the heat diffuser (see page 10) to heat the oil over low heat, increasing the temperature to medium after a few minutes. Do not use on high heat.

Once the oil is hot, sear each chop for about 1-2 minutes or until lightly browned and then remove. Place the orange juice, honey, salt, brown sugar and orange zest in the stoneware. Cover with the seared chops, overlapping them, if necessary. Turn each chop to coat thoroughly with the sauce. Transfer the stoneware to the heating base unit. Cover and cook on High setting 1 to 2 hours or on Low setting for 4 to 5 hours.

Remove the chops to a warmed plate and transfer the remaining liquid to a small, heavy saucepan. Heat the liquid over medium high heat until the liquids begin to boil. In a small bowl, combine the cornstarch and water. Blend well and add to the orange sauce, stirring to mix together the sauce completely. Reduce the heat and simmer for 5 minutes. To serve, spoon the sauce over the chops and serve at once. Serves 8.

Spicy Mexican Pork and Beans

2 tablespoons Spanish olive oil
3 pounds boneless pork butt, trimmed of excess fat
salt and ground black pepper to taste
1 large Spanish onion, peeled and chopped
3 garlic cloves, minced
1 teaspoon ground cumin
1 teaspoon dried oregano
3/4 cup water
1/2 cup applesauce
1 1/2 cups pinto beans, soaked overnight and drained
3 tablespoons green chili peppers, finely chopped
2 tablespoons cilantro leaves, finely chopped

If using a Gas stove, add the oil to the ETC™ stoneware and heat over low heat, increasing the temperature to medium after a few minutes. Do not use on high heat.

If using an Electric stove, use the ETC™ stoneware with the heat diffuser (see page 10) to heat the oil over low heat, increasing the temperature to medium after a few minutes. Do not use on high heat.

Preheat the oven to 325°F.

Season the pork on all sides with salt and pepper. Once the oil is hot, brown the pork 1 to 2 minutes on each side. Add the onion, garlic, cumin, and oregano and cook an additional 3 to 4 minutes until the onion softens. Combine with the water, applesauce, beans and chili peppers in the stoneware. Stir to combine ingredients, cover and braise in the oven 1½ to 2 hours until internal temperature of meat reaches 150°F or desired doneness. Remove the pork from sauce and let rest on a cutting board for at least 15 minutes. Slice and serve with beans and pan sauce. Garnish with cilantro. Makes 6 servings.

Asian Ginger Beef over Bok Choy

2 tablespoons peanut oil
1 1/2 pounds boneless beef chuck roast, cut into 1-inch pieces
3 green onions, cut into 1/2-inch slices
6 cloves garlic
2 teaspoons ground ginger
1 teaspoon Asian chile paste
1/2 cup water
1 cup chicken broth
1/4 cup soy sauce
9 ounces fresh udon noodles, cooked and drained
    (you may substitute vermicelli noodles, if desired)
3 cups bok choy, trimmed, washed and cut into 1-inch pieces
1/2 cup fresh cilantro, minced

If using a Gas stove, add the oil to the ETC™ stoneware and heat over low heat, increasing the temperature to medium after a few minutes. Do not use on high heat.

If using an Electric stove, use the ETC™ stoneware with the heat diffuser (see page 10) to heat the oil over low heat, increasing the temperature to medium after a few minutes. Do not use on high heat.

Once the oil is hot, sear 4 or 5 pieces of beef at a time on all sides, turning each piece as it browns. Sear the last batch of beef with the onions and garlic. Place all of the seared beef in the stoneware along with the ginger, chile paste, water, chicken broth and soy sauce. Stir well to combine the ingredients. Transfer the stoneware to the heating base unit. Cover and cook on High setting for 2 to 4 hours or on Low setting for 6 to 8 hours, or until the beef is very tender.

Just prior to serving, add the noodles to the beef and stir well. Add the bok choy to the beef and noodles and stir again. Heat on High setting until the bok choy is tender-crisp, about 15 minutes. Garnish the beef with the cilantro and serve while hot. Serves 6 to 8.

Shellfish & Chorizo Spanish Paella

2 tablespoons extra virgin olive oil
1 pound Chorizo sausages, casings removed
1 green pepper, chopped
1 medium red onion, chopped
4 cloves garlic, minced
1/2 teaspoon crushed red pepper flakes
2 1/2 cups long-grain white rice
2 cups bottled clam juice
1 cup tomato juice
1/2 cup water
1 cup dry white wine
1/4 teaspoon ground turmeric
1/4 teaspoon freshly ground black pepper
1 teaspoon salt
1/2 teaspoon dried basil
11 1/2 ounce can artichoke hearts, drained
12 small hard-shell clams in the shell, rinsed and scrubbed
1 pound medium-size raw shrimp, shelled and deveined
1 pound cooked crab legs, in the shell, cracked

If using a Gas stove, add the oil to the ETC™ stoneware and heat over low heat, increasing the temperature to medium after a few minutes. Do not use on high heat.

If using an Electric stove, use the ETC™ stoneware with the heat diffuser (see page 10) to heat the oil over low heat, increasing the temperature to medium after a few minutes. Do not use on high heat.

Once the oil is hot, brown and crumble the sausage until no pink remains, about 10 minutes. Drain any fat that accumulates. Combine all of the ingredients except the shellfish in the stoneware and stir to blend well. Transfer the stoneware to the heating base unit and heat on High setting. Cover and cook for 2 to 3 hours, stirring twice.

Thirty minutes before serving, add the clams and shrimp on top of the paella. Arrange the crab legs on top of the other shellfish and cover again. Set the heating base unit on the High setting until the clams pop open, about 20 to 30 minutes. Discard any unopened clams. To serve, ladle equal portions of the paella into large bowls and serve while hot. Serves 6 to 8.

Braised Beef Brisket

2 tablespoons extra virgin olive oil
3-4 pound beef brisket
salt and ground black pepper
5 garlic cloves, minced
1 large yellow onion, diced
1 cup red wine
1 cup beef stock
1/4 cup tomato paste
1 teaspoon dried thyme leaves
2 dried bay leaves
1 teaspoon dried rosemary
2 pounds Yukon Gold potatoes, peeled and cut into 3/4-
    inch cubes
1 pound parsnips, peeled and cut into 1/4-inch slices
1 pound carrots, peeled and cut into 1/4-inch slices

If using a Gas stove, add the oil to the ETC™ stoneware and heat over low heat, increasing the temperature to medium after a few minutes. Do not use on high heat.

If using an Electric stove, use the ETC™ stoneware with the heat diffuser (see page 10) to heat the oil over low heat, increasing the temperature to medium after a few minutes. Do not use on high heat.

Preheat the oven to 300°F.

Season the brisket with salt and pepper. Once the oil is hot, brown the brisket on each side with the garlic and onions, about 2 to 3 minutes per side. Place all of the ingredients in the stoneware. Stir to combine the ingredients and cover. Braise in the oven 2½ to 3 hours until the meat is cooked through and tender. Remove the bay leaves before slicing and serving. Makes 6 servings.

Sauerbraten with Tender Vegetables

2 cups cider vinegar
1 cup water
1 teaspoon salt
1 tablespoon whole black peppercorns
2 dried bay leaves
1 teaspoon whole cloves
3 garlic cloves, crushed
3-4 pounds beef rump roast, trimmed of excess fat
2 tablespoons extra virgin olive oil
2 pounds new potatoes, washed, cut into halves
1 pound carrots, peeled and cut into 1/4 inch slices
2 medium yellow onions, quartered

In a large, self-sealing bag, combine the vinegar, water, salt, peppercorns, bay leaves, cloves and garlic. Stir to combine the ingredients. Add the beef, seal the bag and refrigerate on a tray or plate for 2-3 days, turning the bag occasionally.

If using a Gas stove, add the oil to the ETC™ stoneware and heat over low heat, increasing the temperature to medium after a few minutes. Do not use on high heat.

If using an Electric stove, use the ETC™ stoneware with the heat diffuser (see page 10) to heat the oil over low heat, increasing the temperature to medium after a few minutes. Do not use on high heat.

Preheat the oven to 300°F.

Remove the meat from the marinade and lightly pat dry. Strain and reserve 2 cups of the marinade. Once the oil is hot, brown the roast 2 to 3 minutes per side. Combine the potatoes, carrots, onions, and reserved marinade along with the meat in the stoneware. Cover and braise in the oven 2½ to 3 hours or until cooked to desired doneness. Remove the meat and slice against the grain. Serve with potatoes, vegetables, and accumulated sauce. Makes 6 servings.

Sauvignon Blanc Beef with Beets & Thyme

---

2 tablespoons extra virgin olive oil
3 pounds beef chuck roast
1 medium yellow onion, peeled and quartered
2 cloves garlic, minced
1 pound red or yellow beets, scrubbed and quartered
5 sprigs fresh thyme
1 whole bay leaf
2 whole cloves
1 cup chicken broth
1 cup Sauvignon Blanc
2 tablespoons tomato paste
salt and freshly ground pepper to taste

If using a Gas stove, add the oil to the ETC™ stoneware and heat over low heat, increasing the temperature to medium after a few minutes. Do not use on high heat.

If using an Electric stove, use the ETC™ stoneware with the heat diffuser (see page 10) to heat the oil over low heat, increasing the temperature to medium after a few minutes. Do not use on high heat.

Once the oil is hot, sear the roast with the onions and garlic on both sides for 4-5 minutes, or until it is well-browned. Remove the roast to a large platter.

Place the stoneware on the heating base unit. Layer the beets evenly in the stoneware. Place the roast and onions on top of the beets. Add the thyme, bay leaf and cloves. In a medium bowl, whisk together the broth, Sauvignon Blanc and tomato paste until smooth. Add the salt and pepper to taste and pour over the roast and beets. Cover and cook on High setting 2 to 4 hours or on Low setting for 5 to 7 hours, or until the roast is fork-tender and the beets are softened. Serves 6.

Roast Ham with Tangy Mustard Glaze

3 pounds fully cooked boneless ham, visible fat removed
1/2 teaspoon ground allspice
1/4 cup dark brown sugar, packed
1 tablespoon Dijon mustard
3 tablespoons freshly squeezed lemon juice
1/4 cup sugar
2 tablespoons cornstarch

Place the ham in the ETC™ stoneware. In a small mixing bowl, combine the allspice, brown sugar, mustard and 2 teaspoons of the lemon juice. Spoon the mustard sauce evenly over the ham. Cover and cook in the heating base unit on High setting 2 to 4 hours or on Low setting for 5 to 7 hours, or until the ham is warm throughout and the sauce is well absorbed in the ham. Transfer the ham to a warm serving platter.

Transfer the juices from the stoneware to a small, heavy saucepan along with the lemon juice, sugar, and cornstarch. Heat over medium high heat until the mixture boils. As soon as the sauce boils, reduce to medium heat and stir until the sauce is thickened and glossy. Carve the ham into slices and spoon the sauce over the individual servings. Serves 8 to 10.

Tangerine Broccoli Beef

2 pounds boneless beef top sirloin steak, cut into thin
strips
1 red bell pepper, seeded and sliced into strips
2 cloves garlic, minced
1 tablespoon fresh ginger, grated
1/2 teaspoon crushed red pepper
1 tablespoon soy sauce
2 tablespoons rice vinegar
1 tablespoon oyster sauce
1/4 cup dry sherry
2 cups broccoli florets
1 1/2 tablespoons cornstarch
2 tablespoons water
2 – 8 ounce cans tangerine segments, drained
1/2 cup green onions, thinly sliced
4 cups sticky short-grain white rice, cooked to package
instructions

Combine the steak, pepper, garlic, ginger, red pepper, soy sauce, rice vinegar, oyster sauce and sherry in the ETC™ stoneware. Cover and cook in the heating base unit on High setting for 3 to 5 hours or on Low setting for 7 to 9 hours.

During the last 30 minutes of cooking, add the broccoli florets and stir. Combine the cornstarch and water in a small bowl and add to the juice in the stoneware. Stir as the sauce thickens. Replace the cover and finish cooking. When done, toss the steak with the tangerine segments and green onions. Serve over the white rice. Makes 6 servings.

Gingered Sherry Pork Roast

2 tablespoons extra virgin olive oil
1 clove garlic, chopped
2 1/2 pounds pork roast
12 baby carrots
1 cup snow pea pods
3 green onions, thinly sliced
1 cup sherry
3 tablespoons hoisin sauce
1 tablespoon soy sauce
2 teaspoons fresh ground ginger
1/4 teaspoon fresh ground black pepper
2 tablespoons fresh chives, chopped

If using a Gas stove, add the oil to the ETC™ stoneware and heat over low heat, increasing the temperature to medium after a few minutes. Do not use on high heat.

If using an Electric stove, use the ETC™ stoneware with the heat diffuser (see page 10) to heat the oil over low heat, increasing the temperature to medium after a few minutes. Do not use on high heat.

Once the oil is hot, add the pork roast and sear each side of the meat until golden brown, about 3-4 minutes per side. Remove the roast and set aside.

Transfer the stoneware to the heating base unit and add the carrots, pea pods and onions. In a small bowl, whisk together the sherry, hoisin sauce, soy sauce, ground ginger and the black pepper. Place the seared pork roast on top of the vegetables and pour the sherry sauce over the top. Cover and cook on High setting for 2 to 4 hours or on Low setting for 5 to 7 hours. Baste occasionally with the sherry sauce.

To serve, remove the roast and let it stand for 10 minutes. Slice the pork roast and return it to the stoneware with the vegetables and sauce. Garnish individual servings with the chives. Serves 4.

Shrimp Provençal with Angel Hair Pasta

2 tablespoons extra virgin olive oil
1 small onion, chopped
1 clove garlic, minced
4 large ripe tomatoes, chopped
1 teaspoon dried basil
3/4 cup dry white wine
1 cup chicken broth
salt and ground black pepper to taste
2 pounds large shrimp, peeled and deveined
3/4 pound angel hair pasta, cooked al dente
1/4 cup Italian parsley, chopped

If using a Gas stove, add the oil, onions, and garlic to the ETC™ stoneware and sauté over low heat. Do not use on high heat.

If using an Electric stove, use the ETC™ stoneware with the heat diffuser (see page 10) to sauté the oil, onions, and garlic over low heat. Do not use on high heat.

Sauté the vegetables for about 7 to 8 minutes or until onions are soft and translucent. Transfer the stoneware to the heating base unit and add the tomatoes, basil, wine, chicken broth, salt and pepper. Cover and cook on High setting for 1 to 3 hours or on Low setting for 3½ to 5 hours.

Five to ten minutes before serving, add the shrimp and turn to High setting. To serve, add the cooked pasta and mix well. Sprinkle with the Italian parsley and serve immediately. Serves 4 to 6.

Wild Rice & Almond-Stuffed Game Hens

3/4 cup wild rice, cooked to package instructions
1/2 cup almonds, slivered
1/4 cup shallots, minced
1/2 teaspoon orange zest
2 - 1 1/2 pound game hens, rinsed and dried
1 tablespoon olive oil
1 tablespoon butter
1 1/2 cups beef broth
3/4 cup dry red wine
1 1/2 tablespoons Dijon mustard
3/4 teaspoon dried basil
1/4 teaspoon ground black pepper

Once the rice is cooked, stir in the almonds, shallots and orange zest. Stuff the two prepared game hens with the stuffing.

If using a Gas stove, add the oil and butter to the ETC™ stoneware and heat over low heat, increasing the temperature to medium after a few minutes. Do not use on high heat.

If using an Electric stove, use the ETC™ stoneware with the heat diffuser (see page 10) to heat the oil and butter over low heat, increasing the temperature to medium after a few minutes. Do not use on high heat.

Once the butter and oil are hot, add the game hens and sear them on all sides to brown. Transfer the stoneware to the heating base unit. Whisk together the beef broth, red wine, Dijon mustard, basil and black pepper and pour over the game hens. Cover and cook on the High setting for 1½ to 3 hours or on Low setting for 3 to 5 hours. Drizzle the natural juices over the game hens to serve. Serves 2.

Niku Jaga (Japanese Beef Stew)

2 tablespoons vegetable oil
2 pounds beef stew meat, cut in 1-inch cubes
1 cup water
1/2 cup Japanese sake (or dry white wine)
1/4 cup sugar
1/4 cup soy sauce
1 teaspoon salt
4 medium carrots, peeled and sliced
3 medium Yukon Gold potatoes, peeled and chopped
1 white onion, peeled and chopped
1 tablespoon cornstarch
1/4 cup cold water

If using a Gas stove, add the oil to the ETC™ stoneware and heat over low heat, increasing the temperature to medium after a few minutes. Do not use on high heat.

If using an Electric stove, use the ETC™ stoneware with the heat diffuser (see page 10) to heat the oil over low heat, increasing the temperature to medium after a few minutes. Do not use on high heat.

Once the oil is hot, sear 4 or 5 pieces of beef at a time on all sides, turning as each piece browns. Transfer the stoneware to the heating base unit. Add all of the remaining ingredients except the cornstarch and water and mix well. Cover and cook on High setting for 2 to 4 hours or on Low setting for 5 to 7 hours. Half an hour before cooking is complete, use a small bowl to dissolve the cornstarch into the water. Stir this mixture into the soup and cook for the remaining time. Serves 6 to 8.

St. Patrick's Day
Corned Beef & Cabbage

6 small new potatoes, quartered
2 medium carrots, peeled and thickly sliced
1 1/2 to 2 pounds corned beef brisket
1 medium yellow onion, cut into eighths
3 bay leaves
8 whole black peppercorns
1/2 head green cabbage, cored and cut into wedges

Place the potatoes and carrots in the bottom of the ETC™stoneware. Cover with the beef brisket and place the onion, bay leaves and peppercorns on top. Add enough water to cover the brisket. Place the stoneware in the heating base unit. Cover and cook on High setting for 3 to 5 hours or on Low setting 7 to 10 hours. Halfway through cooking, add the cabbage wedges. Serves 5.

4

Side Dishes

Roasted Summer Squash with Pine Nuts & Romano Cheese

---

2 tablespoons extra virgin olive oil
1 clove garlic, minced
1/2 cup yellow onion, chopped
1 medium red bell pepper, seeded and chopped
3 medium zucchini, cut in 1/2-inch slices
3 medium summer squash, cut in 1/2-inch slices
1/2 cup pine nuts, chopped
1/3 cup Romano cheese, freshly grated
1 teaspoon dried Italian seasoning
1 teaspoon salt, divided
1/4 teaspoon black pepper
1 tablespoon unsalted butter, cut into small cubes

If using a Gas stove, add the oil, garlic, onions and red bell pepper to the ETC™ stoneware and sauté over low heat. Do not use on high heat.

If using an Electric stove, use the ETC™ stoneware with the heat diffuser (see page 10) to sauté the oil, garlic, onions and red bell pepper over low heat. Do not use on high heat.

Stir the vegetables occasionally and sauté until the onions are translucent and soft, about 10 minutes. Transfer the stoneware to the heating base unit. Add the zucchini and summer squash and toss lightly.

In a small bowl, mix together the pine nuts, cheese, Italian seasoning, salt and the pepper. Fold half of the cheese and nuts into the mixture in the stoneware and sprinkle the remaining cheese and nuts on top. Dot the top of the cheese with the butter. Cover and cook on High setting for 1½ to 2 hours or on Low setting for 3 to 5 hours. Serves 6 to 8.

Spring Vegetable Rice Medley

5 ounces frozen chopped spinach, thawed and drained
2 cups converted white rice
4 cups vegetable broth
1 green pepper, seeded and chopped
1 medium ripe tomato, sliced into wedges
1 medium yellow onion, chopped
1 medium carrot, peeled and diced
3 cloves garlic, minced
1 tablespoon Italian parsley, minced
1 teaspoon salt
1/2 teaspoon freshly ground black pepper
13 3/4 ounce can artichoke hearts, quartered, rinsed and
      well-drained
1/2 cup frozen peas

Combine the spinach, rice, vegetable broth, green pepper, tomato, onion, carrot, garlic, parsley, salt and pepper in the ETC™ stoneware. Mix thoroughly. Cover and cook on High setting for 2 hours or on Low setting for 4 hours. Add the artichoke hearts and peas to the stoneware 15 minutes prior to serving. Cover and continue cooking. Mix again just before serving. Serves 8.

Burgundy & Wild Crimini Mushroom Pilaf

2 tablespoons vegetable oil
2 cups converted white rice
1 medium onion, chopped
1 cup wild crimini mushrooms, sliced
1 small zucchini, thinly sliced
4 cups beef or vegetable broth
1/2 cup burgundy (or other deep, full-bodied wine)
1/2 teaspoon salt
1/4 teaspoon freshly ground black pepper
4 tablespoons butter, melted

If using a Gas stove, add the oil to the ETC™ stoneware and heat over low heat, increasing the temperature to medium after a few minutes. Do not use on high heat.

If using an Electric stove, use the ETC™ stoneware with the heat diffuser (see page 10) to heat the oil over low heat, increasing the temperature to medium after a few minutes. Do not use on high heat.

Once the oil is hot, add the rice, onion, mushrooms and zucchini. Stir to combine the ingredients and sauté for 4–5 minutes until the rice is slightly browned and onions are soft. Transfer the stoneware to the heating base unit.

Pour the beef broth and burgundy over the rice mixture. Season with the salt and pepper and drizzle the melted butter over all. Stir once. Cover and cook on Low setting for 3 to 5 hours until all the liquid has been absorbed, stirring twice during the cooking process. Serves 6.

Mango Spiced Ribs

2 tablespoons vegetable oil
3 pounds beef short ribs
1 cup mango chutney
1 clove garlic, minced
1 teaspoon curry powder
1/2 teaspoon ground cinnamon
1/2 teaspoon salt

If using a Gas stove, add the oil to the ETC™ stoneware and heat over low heat, increasing the temperature to medium after a few minutes. Do not use on high heat.

If using an Electric stove, use the ETC™ stoneware with the heat diffuser (see page 10) to heat the oil over low heat, increasing the temperature to medium after a few minutes. Do not use on high heat.

Once the oil is hot, add a few ribs at a time to sear and brown the beef on all sides, about 1 to 2 minutes per side. Transfer the stoneware to the heating base unit. Add the remaining ingredients and mix well. Cover and cook on High setting for 2 to 4 hours or on Low setting for 5 to 7 hours, turning the ribs in the sauce occasionally. Makes 12 appetizer servings.

Creamy Curried Spinach

3 – 10 ounce pkgs. frozen spinach, thawed
1 large yellow onion, chopped
4 cloves garlic, minced
2 tablespoons curry powder
2 tablespoons butter, melted
1/4 cup chicken broth
1/4 cup heavy cream
1 teaspoon lemon juice

Combine the spinach, onion, garlic, curry powder, butter and chicken broth in the ETC™ stoneware. Cover and cook on High setting for 2 hours or on Low setting for 3 to 4 hours. Thirty minutes before serving, add the cream and lemon juice. Stir well to blend and continue cooking for remainder of the time. Serves 8.

Honey-Glazed Chicken Wings

3 tablespoons vegetable oil
3 pounds chicken wings, tips removed
1 teaspoon freshly ground pepper
1 cup clover honey
1/2 cup soy sauce
1 clove garlic, minced
2 tablespoons tomato paste
1 teaspoon sugar
2 teaspoons water

If using a Gas stove, add the oil to the ETC™ stoneware and heat over low heat, increasing the temperature to medium after a few minutes. Do not use on high heat.

If using an Electric stove, use the ETC™ stoneware with the heat diffuser (see page 10) to heat the oil over low heat, increasing the temperature to medium after a few minutes. Do not use on high heat.

Season the wings with pepper. Once the oil is hot, brown 3 to 4 of the chicken wings at a time on each side, about 1 to 2 minutes per side. Remove chicken with a slotted spoon and continue browning until all chicken is browned. Place all of the browned chicken in the stoneware.

In a medium bowl, combine the honey, soy sauce and the garlic. Whisk in the tomato paste, sugar and water. Transfer the stoneware to the heating base unit.

Pour the honey mixture over the chicken. Cover and cook on High setting for 1 to 2 hours or on Low setting for 2 to 4 hours. Serves 6 to 8.

Fresh Pizza or Pasta Sauce

2 tablespoons vegetable oil
1 medium red onion, peeled and diced
1 clove garlic, minced
3 1/2 cups vine ripe tomatoes, peeled and chopped
12 ounce can tomato puree
6 ounce can tomato paste
1/4 cup dry red wine
2 tablespoons fresh parsley, chopped
1 tablespoon fresh oregano, chopped
1/2 teaspoon salt
1/4 teaspoon freshly ground pepper

If using a Gas stove, add the oil, onions, and garlic to the ETC™ stoneware and sauté over low heat. Do not use on high heat.

If using an Electric stove, use the ETC™ stoneware with the heat diffuser (see page 10) to sauté the oil, onions, and garlic over low heat. Do not use on high heat.

Sauté for about 7 to 8 minutes or until onions are soft and translucent. Transfer the stoneware to the heating base unit and add the tomatoes, tomato puree, tomato paste, wine, parsley, oregano, salt and pepper. Cover and cook on High setting for 1 to 3 hours or on Low setting for 3 to 5 hours.

Creamy Red Pepper Polenta

4 tablespoons butter, melted
1/4 teaspoon ground paprika
1/8 teaspoon cayenne pepper
1/8 teaspoon ground cumin
6 cups water, heated to boiling
2 cups yellow cornmeal
1 small red bell pepper, seeded and finely chopped
2 teaspoons salt

Combine the butter, paprika, cayenne and cumin in the ETC™ stoneware. Add the hot water, cornmeal, red pepper and salt and stir well to blend. Transfer the stoneware to the heating base unit. Cover and cook on High setting for 1 to 2 hours or on Low setting for 3 to 4 hours, stirring occasionally. Serves 4 to 6.

Wild Rice with Mushrooms

---

2 tablespoons extra virgin olive oil
1/4 cup sweet onion, minced
3 cups chicken or vegetable broth
1/4 teaspoon onion powder
1 1/2 cups white button mushrooms, cleaned, stems
    removed and diced
1 cup brown rice, uncooked
7 ounce pkg. wild rice mix
salt and pepper to taste

If using a Gas stove, heat the oil in the ETC™ stoneware on low on the stove. Add the onions and sauté until they are softened. Do not use the ETC™ on high heat.

If using an Electric stove, use the ETC™ stoneware with the heat diffuser (see page 10) to heat the oil over low heat. Add the onions and sauté until they are softened. Do not use on high heat.

Stir the onions occasionally and cook until they are translucent and soft, about 5-6 minutes. Incorporate all of the ingredients into the stoneware and transfer to the heating base unit. Cover and cook on High setting for 1 to 3 hours or on Low setting for 3 to 5 hours, or until the rice is tender and the broth is absorbed. Season with salt and pepper to taste. Serves 6 to 8.

Gratin Potatoes with Asiago Cheese

6 slices bacon, cut into 1 inch pieces
6 medium baking potatoes, peeled and thinly sliced
1/2 cup Asiago cheese, freshly grated
salt and pepper to taste
1 1/2 cups heavy cream

If using a Gas stove, use the ETC™ stoneware to sauté the bacon on low for a few minutes and then turn the heat up to medium for about 10 minutes until crisp. Do not use on high heat.

If using an Electric stove, use the ETC™ stoneware with the heat diffuser (see page 10) to sauté the bacon until crisp over medium low heat. Do not use on high heat.

Remove the bacon with a slotted spoon and set aside on a paper towel to drain. Transfer the stoneware with the bacon fat to the heating base unit. Layer one-fourth of the potatoes on the bottom of the stoneware. Sprinkle one-fourth of the bacon over the potatoes and top with one-fourth of the cheese. Salt and pepper to taste. Continue layering until all of the potatoes, bacon and cheese are used. Pour the cream over all. Cover and cook on High setting for 1 to 3 hours or on Low setting for 3 to 5 hours. Adjust the seasonings to taste. Serves 4 to 6.

Oriental Golden Barley with Cashews

---

2 tablespoons unsalted butter
1 cup hulled barley, sorted
3 cups vegetable broth
1/4 teaspoon finely ground black pepper
1 clove garlic, minced
1 cup celery, chopped
1 green bell pepper, seeded and chopped
1 yellow onion, peeled and minced
1/4 cup cashews, finely chopped

If using a Gas stove, heat the oil and barley in the ETC™ stoneware on low on the stove. Do not use on high heat.
If using an Electric stove, use the ETC™ stoneware with the heat diffuser (see page 10) to heat the oil and barley over low heat. Do not use on high heat.

Sauté the barley for about ten minutes or until slightly browned. Transfer the stoneware to the heating base unit. Add the vegetable broth, pepper, garlic, celery, bell pepper and onion and blend well. Cover and cook on High setting 1 to 3 hours or on Low setting for 3 to 5 hours. The barley and vegetables will be tender and the liquid absorbed when the dish is ready to serve. Garnish each serving with the cashews. Serves 4.

Warm Artichoke Cheese Spread with Flatbread

1 pound mozzarella cheese, shredded
1 cup Parmesan cheese, grated
1 cup mayonnaise
1 cup artichoke hearts, drained and chopped
1 red pepper, seeded and finely chopped
2 cloves garlic, minced
8 pieces flatbread

Place all of the ingredients except the flatbread in the ETC™ stoneware and mix thoroughly. Cover and cook on High setting for 1 to 2 hours. Mix again and turn the heat setting to Warm. Serve the cheese spread in the stoneware. Pass pieces of the flatbread to each guest. Guests may tear small portions of the bread to dip in the spread. Serves 8.

5

Desserts

Spiced Apple, Oatmeal & Vanilla Cream Buckle

1 cup rolled oats, toasted
1/3 cup dark brown sugar, packed
8 green apples, cored, peeled, and thinly sliced
1 1/4 teaspoon ground cinnamon
1/4 teaspoon ground allspice
1/4 teaspoon ground nutmeg
1/8 teaspoon ground cloves
1 cup heavy cream
2 tablespoons unsalted butter, softened
1/2 cup sugar
2 eggs
2 teaspoons vanilla extract
1/2 cup prepared biscuit baking mix
1 tablespoon butter or margarine
2 cups vanilla bean ice cream

In a small bowl, combine the toasted oats with the brown sugar and stir to thoroughly combine. Place the ETC™ stoneware in the heating base unit and coat the stoneware lightly with nonstick cooking spray. Place the apples, cinnamon, allspice, nutmeg and cloves in the stoneware and toss lightly.

In a medium bowl, combine the cream, butter, sugar, eggs, vanilla and the biscuit baking mix. Stir until fairly smooth and spoon over the spiced apples. Sprinkle with the toasted oats and sugar and dot with the butter. Cover and cook on High setting for 2 to 4 hours, or until the apples are very soft and the topping is slightly firm. Spoon while warm into individual bowls and garnish each serving with a scoop of vanilla bean ice cream. Makes 6 to 8 servings.

Slow-Roasted Plantains
with Rum Sauce

---

6 plantains or bananas, ripe and soft
1/2 cup sugar
1/4 cup dark brown sugar
1/2 teaspoon ground cinnamon
1/4 cup dark rum
1/4 cup fresh orange juice
1/4 cup unsalted butter, cut into small pieces

Coat the ETC™ stoneware with nonstick cooking spray. Peel and slice the plantains into ½-inch thick slices. Place the plantain slices in the stoneware in even layers. Sprinkle the sugars and cinnamon over the plantains. Drizzle the rum and orange juice over all and top with the pieces of butter. Cover and cook on High setting for 1 to 3 hours, or until the plantains are golden and the sauce is warm throughout. Cool for 10 minutes and serve over ice cream or cake. Serves 8.

Coconut & Spiced Apple Dessert

5 tart baking apples, peeled and coarsely sliced
1/4 cup coconut, sweetened and flaked
1/4 cup macadamia nuts, finely chopped
1 tablespoon all purpose flour
1/3 cup dark brown sugar, packed
1/2 teaspoon ground cinnamon
1/2 teaspoon ground nutmeg
1/8 teaspoon ground cardamom
1/2 cup butterscotch chips, melted
1/3 cup all purpose flour
1/2 cup rolled oats (regular or quick-cooking)
2 tablespoons butter
whipped cream for garnish

Combine the apples, coconut, nuts, 1 tablespoon flour, brown sugar, cinnamon, nutmeg, and cardamom in the ETC™ stoneware. Blend well. Drizzle with the melted butterscotch chips. In a separate bowl, combine the flour, oats and butter. Cut with a pastry cutter until the mixture is crumbly and sprinkle over the apples. Cover and cook on High setting for 1 to 3 hours or on Low setting for 3 to 5 hours. Serve warm with homemade whipped cream. Serves 4.

Hawaiian Fruit Compote

---

3 grapefruits, peeled and sectioned
2 to 3 limes, peeled and sectioned
3 cups fresh pineapple, coarsely chopped
2 cups peaches, pitted and chopped
1 mango, peeled and chopped
2 bananas, peeled and sliced
1 tablespoon lemon juice
21 ounce can cherry pie filling
slivered almonds, toasted, for garnish

Place all of the fruit and the cherry pie filling in the ETC™ stoneware and toss lightly. Cover and cook on High setting for 1 to 3 hours or on Low setting for 3 to 5 hours. Transfer to serving dishes and top with the almonds to garnish. Serves 6 to 8.

Cinnamon Ginger Poached Pears

---

3 cups water
1 cup granulated sugar
10 slices fresh ginger
2 whole cinnamon sticks
6 Bosc or Anjou pears, peeled and cored
1 tablespoon candied ginger for garnish

Combine the water, sugar, fresh ginger and cinnamon sticks in the ETC™ stoneware and set on heating base unit. Add the pears. Cover and cook on High setting for 1½ to 2 hours or on Low setting for 3 to 6 hours. Remove the pears from the sauce and cool slightly. Turn the heat setting to High and cook the sauce until thickened, about 30 minutes. Drizzle the sauce over the pears to serve. Garnish with the candied ginger. Serves 4.

Classic Baked Apples

---

2 tablespoons golden raisins
1/4 cup dark brown sugar, packed
1 teaspoon lemon zest, grated
6 small to medium baking apples, washed and cored
1 teaspoon ground cinnamon
2 tablespoons butter
1/4 cup orange juice
1/4 cup water
whipped cream for garnish

Mix together in a small bowl the raisins, sugar and lemon zest. Fill the core of each apple with the raisins and sugar. Place the apples in the ETC™ stoneware and sprinkle with the cinnamon and dot with butter. Pour the orange juice and water over the apples. Cover and cook on High setting for 2½ to 3½ hours or on Low setting for 5 to 7 hours. To serve, remove the apples from the sauce and place in individual bowls. Top with the remaining sauce in the stoneware and the whipped cream to garnish. Makes 4 servings.

Sparkling Mango-Wine Granita

---

1 1/4 cups water, boiling
1/2 cup sugar
3 1/2 cups fresh mango, cubed
2 teaspoons lime juice
3 cups dry white wine
lime zest for garnish

Combine the boiling water and sugar in the ETC™ stoneware and stir until the sugar dissolves. Transfer the stoneware to the heating base unit. Add the mangos and the lime juice and stir to blend. Cover and cook on High setting for 1 hour. Cool slightly and place the mangos and ½ cup of the cooking syrup in a food processor or blender. Puree and cool completely.

In the stoneware, combine the mango puree, wine and the remaining cooking syrup until blended. Cover the stoneware and place it in the freezer for 2 hours. Remove the frozen granita from the freezer, mash gently and return it to the freezer for another 2 hours.

To serve, remove the granita from the freezer 15 minutes before serving. Scoop out individual servings into champagne glasses and top each with a garnish of lime zest. Serves 6.